AF751652

From poems of desire and sexual longing to poems of love in the face of death, *The Cyprian* explores the joy and heartbreak love weaves into our lives. The collection confronts some of our primary questions about love: how is it possible to accept the death of the beloved? What role does deception play in love? When does love become a force of exploitation? The collection is composed of five parts, reflecting different aspects of Aphrodite, the goddess of love and beauty – a complexity which is also implicit in the ambiguity of the book's title, 'the Cyprian'.

Crutchfield trained as a classicist, and her poetry combines conversational idioms with mythic visions of human relationship, 'longing and its / fierce metamorphosis'. Elegies, love poems and imagistic snapshots mix with wide open epistolary verse. Her poetry reclaims the linguistic power and range of allusion found in late romantic poets like Christopher Brennan and Francis Webb, bringing them to bear on contemporary female experience.

Crutchfield brings the mythic into contact with the quotidian, using Aphrodite to explore women's loves, needs and losses...
Winner, Prime Minister's Literary Award for Poetry 2024

AMY CRUTCHFIELD

THE CYPRIAN

NEW POEMS

GIRAMONDO

First published 2023
from the Writing and Society Research Centre
at Western Sydney University
by the Giramondo Publishing Company
PO Box 752
Artarmon NSW 1570 Australia
www.giramondopublishing.com

© Amy Crutchfield 2023

Cover and design by Jenny Grigg
Typesetting by Andrew Davies
in 9/15 pt Tiempos Regular

Printed and bound by SOS Print+Media
Distributed in Australia by NewSouth Books

A catalogue record for this
book is available from the
National Library of Australia.

ISBN: 978-1-922725-77-6

All rights reserved.
No part of this publication may be
reproduced, stored in a retrieval
system or transmitted in any form or
by any means electronic, mechanical,
photocopying or otherwise without the
prior permission of the publisher.

9 8 7 6 5 4 3 2

The Giramondo Publishing Company acknowledges the support
of Western Sydney University in the implementation of its book
publishing program.

This project has been assisted by the Commonwealth Government
through the Australia Council, its arts funding and advisory body.

For my father and in memory of my mother

Contents

Egg 1

Aphrodite Epistrophia – *Who Turns to Love*

He Rises 5

Pothos II 6

Pothos III 7

Dora and the Minotaur (1936) ink, pencil and scratching on paper 8

Camera Obscura 14

Aphrodite Hoplismena – *Armed*

The Memory of Water 17

Helens of Troy 20

Moon Cocoon 22

Pumpkin 23

Yew 24

Aphrodite Pandemos – *Common to All*

A Clean House 29

Market Day 32

MH17 34

Nothing Is Past 36

True in the Senses 37

Aphrodite Ambologera – *Delayer of Old Age*

Alyki 41

A Party on the Coast 43

Beautiful Corpse 44

Half-life 46

The Last Sense 49

Young Women in the Garden, Bonnard (1921–3/1945–6) 50

Young Women in the Garden II/The Colour of Escape 51

Aphrodite Genetyllis – *Protectress of births*

Paper Lantern 55

Skoliosi 56

Undo 57

Child Receding 58

Welcome to the Future of Custom Lightsabers 59

Ob. 60

A Narrow Field 61

Acknowledgements 71

Egg

What shall the mother of the dead be called?
As widow is to wife,
what of the woman left behind?

Like a collector's egg she sits, perfectly
expressionless.

Vessels defined by what they hold.
Heaven without the earth
is air.

Eyes like abandoned corridors.
Ears schooled to sounds none else can hear.

Only the moon can bring dead children home.
Shepherding them across black fields,
driving them out again at dawn.

Aphrodite Epistrophia

Who Turns to Love

He Rises

after Lawrence and Boruch

from the chamber, pale and grand and naked.
His penis is missing and yet I see it,
frail and awry beneath a cloud of hair.
His breast and the pillar of his belly glow
for a *Kandelaber* burns inside him too.
Ambiguity, round-faced, persists. His lips
sit slightly open as if to let
desire escape like breath.
His gaze is lifted, distant. Only longing is left,
pellets of it, in the hollow of him. Recall
his box of sycamore, seven strings of gut,
ten fingers still tender, one dark centre.
Right hip cocked, left leg crossed, heel raised so
his toes rest lightly on the earth, he leans
into space, toward a support
now lost. Who stood beside him?
Was Pothos borne by Love, our ally of the night,
Epistrophia? There is no place I do not see you.

Pothos II

Museo Centrale Montemartini

By lips slightly open and eyes
a little sunken, we might recognise him.
This is the work of Skopas and this figure,
rescued from misnomer, no Apollo
but Pothos – god of longing.
Among the dead he breathes, exhales desire
which moves in waves toward its object.
What did Skopas know of this,
arriving footsore and dusty in Megara,
his chisels in a roll of leather?
Did he catch it in a calm pool of water
or watch it pass as the shadow of a cloud across the plain
face of an apprentice
in the workshops at the growing temple?
What had he learned of longing and its
fierce metamorphosis?
Because the categories are not fixed,
needs jostle on the ladder and we
do not sleep, we do not eat.

Pothos III

The stem moves at its own pace, leans as each
of us leans toward our solace, on sticky
countertops in laneway bars
or the beaded gardens of Mo'orea,
in the bruised light
of the understorey
Epipremnum aureum
tenders itself
toward that brightness –
silver vine,
marble queen,
hunter's robe,
Ceylon creeper
and because
it can survive
in darkness,
Pothos is
Devil's
ivy.

Dora and the Minotaur (1936)
ink, pencil and scratching on paper

1. Les Deux Magots

A rook upon the orchard wall, he spies her gloves.
Pink peonies upon black silk, he stares
as she peels them off.
Painted nails, long fingers splayed, she begins the game.
The pricks are rhythmic, ever faster, too close too close!
She does not halt.
Later he aches –
her Spanish tongue, her solemn bronze,
the columns where he would.

2. Mougins

A breeze plays with the drape, fingers
its linen folds, lifts them and then, lets them subside,
time and again, as if nothing existed beyond
touch and response.

Beside the open glass her nipples harden.
A living marble, she soothes him
to miniature strokes,
sculpted pebbles,
littoral treasures,
a paper pup,
a bird on a wire –
constant tokens of his heart.

Each day with friends on *la terrasse*,
they dine inside a cage the awning casts.
Forested hills tumble down to the Bay of Cannes.
Jasmine, pine, lolling petunia,
ivy sidling ever higher.
At meals his restless fingers find
fantastic beasts inside bottle tops and paper scraps, napkins and wire.
He tears and twists until he draws them out.

Siestas bring their usual swapping.
August too has its cruelties.
She brushes off the grains that creep
into their sheets.

Somewhere in the sands they find
the horned skull with its blank gaze,
she bids him raise it to his face.

3. Minotaur

In the shadow of Guernica, she fought for him,
like a cat on the studio floor,
Marie-Thérèse defending her claim,
Pablo delighted, refusing to choose.

Devilishly seductive with her disguise
of tears and marvellous hats,
she feeds his appetite for anguish,
the drama they both love,
plays his games
laced with cruelty.

The sweetest fish are filled with bones.
Greeks say cats cry to watch us eat them –
the way we suck each bony sickle.
And when one tiny piton lodges in the secret
pink of the gullet –
It will kill us! Until it doesn't. And like a twin,
on the heels of small respite, appetite is born anew.

The heart knows its way
to places where the rules don't hold
and desire betrays us, pipes us
into our degradations.
Or is it the abasement we seek.

What is there that hunger cannot encompass?
Witness the snake, who will dislocate its own jaw – the
    impossible stretch –

At the centre of the universe, a forge.
The heat is *insupportable.*
No fire without fuel,
no flame that does not consume.

He paints her acquiescent beneath
an orange sky.

4. Museum

At the Bar Catalan
she sees the twin birds swoop,
watches him stride
toward Françoise
bearing a bowl of hearts.

What is a goddess when she's forgotten?
First the plinth and then the doormat.
There are not enough museums
for all we once believed in.

Each day she starts
a life after, but not without –
boxes beneath the bed, each drawer, each shelf –
love notes, photos, fragments, jewels,
sketch books, pebbles, oils, nudes

143 lots – *objets d'art, de douleur, de perte.*
Love ends when perspective returns.
Without sight lines, there is no
vanishing point.

A tapered finger against her cheek
bears the oval portrait ring – loose
after fifty years. She hears again the way,
swathed in his Spanish 's'
the sound became   *'Cerisses?'*

Camera Obscura

21 August, 2017

We are not in the path of totality.
For that we would need to be
in Stanley, Idaho, or Casper, Wyoming,
or at least some place with eclipse parking.

Still, we are waiting
and you're walking around with your head in a box
– a cardboard Horus – it's turning me on.
Is it an omen?

In Yin three millennia ago they carved it in a tortoise shell:
three flames
ate the sun
big stars
were seen

Now as then hush descends as the darkness opens.
In an obscure room, sparrow offers
silent greeting to the swallowing moon.

Aphrodite Hoplismena
Armed

The Memory of Water

It occurs to me that I will remember
this time for its inbetweenness
removed from the continuity of things
and it's as if I am a long way off
somewhere else and watching myself...
Al Purdy, 'The Blue City'

We have sailed from Piraeus, left one empire,
not yet at another. The prow noses Thalassa.
The water parts, reassembles. There is no road
and then no wake – churning, then nothing.
Though some say, water has a memory.

Paupers with golden limbs,
our summers stretched like gum,
waiting for something to happen
and then it does. We meet C.

C. has a certain luminescence;
everybody watches, everybody listens.
Joy itself is hypnotic,
a man who knows his bliss
and follows it. Who will stop him?

Rey sought to show that water kept the memory
of an element it had held
long after that element had been removed.
It was a heavy hydrogen.

C. sees me. He even sees me, or seems to,
as I see myself – a very tiny woman.
Which is his secret,
though now it is mine too, and all at once
I know my talent
will not be voice or dance, but something more mithridatic:
to swallow what is dark, then swallow more.
My eyes shall grow but not my tongue.
Port to port, the ship sails on.

Siesta hour felt the most oppressive.
The way adults would expect us to sleep
in stale cabins to rehearse deaths
that belonged to them. While on deck
the blue bore down, and the sun stood ready
to set our lives alight.

We are a long way off
but, watch, there I go.
While everybody else is resting
I hop along the alphabet, our deck
to his.

The eggs of the emerald damsel fly are hatched by heat.
One hundred possible lives,
laid in an open stem or rotting wood.
Wingless nymphs emerge.

Life is a picking up and a setting down.
Through observing we effect the world. And so
I close my eyes. Though at times,
an imprint: in my pleural cavity, a tightening.
Muscles have a memory.
The conscious mind need not participate.

Perhaps C. lives there, in the cells,
somewhere beyond my reach
I walk an airless corridor; he waits to greet me.

I remember most the lotion, which he handled like an unguent,
although it was a common cream.
And I think of church wine, bought in bulk,
the barrels bumping on the bed of a truck.

And a man who waits
to bless it with his touch, believing his intention
has the power to turn one thing into another.

Helens of Troy

We're at a lecture on Helen, he's giving the vote of thanks, when he zeroes in on 3.180 – κυνώπιδος ('kunopidos') – dog-eyed i.e. shameless. Some translators skip it but by Chicago in '51, 'dog-eyed' morphs to 'slut', and it is this rendition he wants to endorse.

I too like to take it in my mouth –
this word 'slut'–
the way the 's' leans into the 'l'
with a strength that sweeps them both
into the cup of its vowel
then sloshes up into that glottal stop.

But when I hear him say it, I smell
the pork shoulder
I bought in the peak of summer
and left a day or two too long –
I know what I know,
and had to throw it.

Escaped or raped, seduced or abducted, beguiler or victim, smart or stupid.
Helen is multiplex. Helene of the many facets, and yet,
diamond is diamond, however you cut it.
Helen is fear. Take the shape of yours, pour her in.

Fear of souls sucked forth
Fear of faces launching ships
Fear of men wearing leopard
Fear of topless towers
Fear of fighting ten years
Fear of fighting ten years, then taking her back
Fear of love, which is not possession
Fear of loyalty, the stem of betrayal
Fear of dogs on heat, who actively seek it
Fear of women being raped
Fear of the urge to rape them

When I hear him say it, I recall
all the sluts I've known, the sluts I've loved,
the sluts within my multitudes – and I sing.
I sing us all, I howl.

Moon Cocoon

6 January, 2021

Anonymous, insatiate, we munch and spin
a thread, thin but strong. *Morus*, it draws us on.
Diminutive monsters, squeezings from giant pores.
Tentacular, we rear and wave, and where one falls
one more will come until we've made our thread.
Captive generations have washed the colour from us,
we grow whiter, wider. Were we allowed wings,
our wings would be too small to lift us out.
We hatch our own death eggs,
our moon cocoons. Our glory is our ruin.

Pumpkin

Stitched to my heel, he followed me in
from the pounding rhythm.
I saw him first when I turned
to lock the door

he had already spread himself against.
6 ft 4 and the strangest thing
that pumpkin grin.
To see me understand – it pleased him.

By way of response I did not
reject him, but smiled.
I smiled from the other side,
with my eyes and with my mouth.

Yew

When I think of yew
I think of those berries
the colour of a glacé cherry
or apples dipped in candy.
The colour of bets we placed, losses
gamblers chase.

The colour of a woman's lips in rouge absolu.
They say we paint our mouths this way
to make them look more like
the box for a defibrillator. Stop me
and start me up again.

The colour of a nosebleed on tissue
or exsanguination, which is red
but also blue. The colour of a heart on fire
like the one Augustine holds high
in Veritas by de Champaigne.

Circle of pleasure, circle of sustenance,
and where they intersect, a lens,
sweet as it is slender.

Yew berries are a pseudofruit.
Fruit found false because it is not born
from the female part transformed.
To manage life with language,

we would call these berries, arils. Beloved
of thrush and waxwing; bright and plump and
wildly toxic.

In the painting by de Champaigne
Augustine sits at his desk beside the window.
He holds his rosy *cor* aloft
as beams of truth ignite it.

Sometimes one ember,
a single wind-borne word, will settle.
The house burns down the same.

When I think of yew
I think of the summer I became one.
I stood in La Haye-de-Routot,
with a hollow inside my trunk
so big they stuck a door on it
and made the chapel of St Anne.
Non sum qualis eram, I am not
as I once was.

Aphrodite Pandemos
Common to All

A Clean House

Cleaning up dog vomit, I wonder
if I really am a dog lover.
A lover of anything. The vomit
an improbable brown only found in hand-knits or
in the kingdom of fungi.
It's grounding.

The sleeves of my robe retentively rolled,
I ask how Shoukei Matsumoto
or the other monks in Kyoto
would approach this task.

The earthly dirt
that accumulates in the soul, poisons your mind,
manifests as a dirty room.
Wipe your floor and see
when you polish the floor you shine
your heart and mind.

Cleaning up vomit reminds me of marriage (mine)
and suicide. Anyone
who'll tell you what's going on
in someone else's marriage is idle, and probably lying.
It reminds me of the time in my marriage
when I had asked,
please,
no new puppy

It reminds me of suicide
because that has its domestic aspect too.
Easy to dismiss,
perhaps,
when you're not the one on your knees
who still has to live in that town,
ask for the bond.

The body, toxic
spasming
ejecta.

Something reptilian
knowing only
to void.

In Jissoin, there is a special word for the floor
polished to a lustre enough to mirror the surrounding leaves –
yuka momiji (autumn leaf floor),
yuka midori (green floor).

Eight hundred years of polishing,
cotton socks,
monks on their knees.
We don't polish the floor because of dirt.

Like an old-time detective, scenting
Prunus amara in the air, announcing –
'Cyanide,' I smelt the bitterness.
'Someone had to clean up.'

Thought how love can turn,
not to less love, but disgust.

In fall, the maples bleed out.
The temple floor, awash with crimson.

Prunus dulcis, the sweet sister, last thing I gave him before he died.
I had jangled in, down from the city,
asked what he wanted from the shops,
with a tone that said – ask me for anything,
please
He asked for a bag of almonds.

Why not polish the floor in your home as if you were polishing a mirror that will reflect your soul.

In winter, the wetblack boards turn white.
Mt Hiei wears a shroud. Fusuma redefine the space:
what was a wall becomes a door,
and, within their painted screen,
red-crowned cranes sky-point and spread their wings.

Market Day

Dawn had just begun to pull upon
the thread of night.

I sensed first your warmth
and then a kiss on my hair.
Brother, I still feel it there.

Then a question, your refrain
each market day since you were eight.
'*Habibti*, my sweet, tell me
what can I bring for you?'

I did not reply: green apples, sweet almonds,
thin-skinned dates.
From sleep's embrace,
I mumbled, '*Wala shee*,' nothing,
and rolled away.

Could I have charged you
with finding something other
than what you sought that morning
in the crowded square?

I arose to the scent of Al-Furat,
life-giving river.
But by noon the window stood
still open and still empty,

admitting only the heat
of Rub'al Khali – *the empty quarter* –
into the room we once shared.

MH17

Speck

Bright insect
inching across the firmament.

First the shock front.
Then the blast wind.

Bodies fall
into an airless sea.

Pixilation

Tiny squares unite to divide.
We are shown an ashen heap

but the seal is not complete.
Here, a pair of legs alone. There

a shoulder with its arm,
and then the hand, fingers spread.

Apron

A flap of the plane's skin
hangs in the forest's canopy.

Another sheet, insignia unfurled,
stands ready to sail across a sea of rippling wheat.

Seats bask in the fields
in clusters of two or three.

Some on their sides,
others facing back up to the sky.

Each chunk of wreckage
with its apron of personal effects.

A suitcase, open-mouthed, allows
a deep pink cardigan to escape.

Turbine

Your blades once sat
snug as gills inside their toadstool cap.

Now skewed and compressed
the blades look like the cutaway

of a chambered nautilus
nestled far from its element.

A shell bound by its ratio,
its beauty chained yet infinite.

Nothing Is Past

My host, a youth, is dead.
Someone unseen inhabits his account, messages me.
A sister, a mother? One who knew
how he loved his *ville Paris, la vie, le sport et la Nature.*

I have seen how a house can decline,
possessions settle into obsolescence.
Here, nothing is past.
This is a space abandoned *tout d'un coup,*
as in violence or war. How many
chambers like these,
just as they were?

In the profile he is blurred, indigo
against a graffitied wall,
the word 'diaspora' in black,
and, at his back, a tornado in mustard
within which two small houses, one carmine,
one azure, spin and lift.

True in the Senses

It is shameful for any man to write in figure and colour and not be able to strip his meaning of such decoration and say plainly what he has in mind.
Charles Williams paraphrasing Dante, *Vita Nuova* xxv

I have always been a liar.
Some years I lied on the page as well – but
the poem won't stand plumb.
Truth is ballast – without these stones
a poem is a pleasure craft, heeling in wind.
And isn't the sixth sense this –
the sense of truth? A sense the heart knows
like we know sour milk. Or is it the hairs
on the body's dial – measuring truth
as they quiver and lift? Knowing
that the only true I mean, is true in the sense
that a heart is not contained by its ribs. True in the sense
of a hammer, sweet on its nail,
pleasure rising
into your wrist. True in the sense that a woman has a smell,
and it is of iron.
True in the sense of the sight of the ghost-
white hair on a goat's neck;
true in the sense of a bleat; and of a knife's edge – *la lame*,
who says what she means and
means what she says.

Aphrodite Ambologera
Delayer of Old Age

Alyki

Paros, Greece

Stelios, in your mountaintop studio
with a view to rival Agamemnon's –
you warned me
'Alyki is not

poetic.'
Your accent was sweet and thick,
a wisp
escaped your shirt and oh,
your glaze! Your celadon insouciance.

To leave you
with your painted plates, your dragonflies and octopi,
is to descend.

You're right, this village isn't much
of anything but earnest.
At night there's nothing here –
the hills swept bare.
Each dawn the whole starts over.

Raw linen, trailed in coffee or black wine,
draws the hills into the sky.
A widow wraps the harbour in foil
and throws a cloth on the sea.
It wrinkles. She shakes it
again, obsessively.

The catch diminishes but not the need.
Still at six the smallest caïques appear.
Perhaps in the shallows a dramatist is caught
as his suckered arm extends
in a flourish of purple from the pale seabed.

A Party on the Coast

When the doctors told her, she threw a party.
'A Night to Remember', the invitation said.

We came in anything but black.
Drank champagne, ate salmon canapés.

There was an almost famous band
and it was too loud to speak.

She smiled all night and watched
the dance floor throb.

Outside the window
the inky sea and then beyond.

Beautiful Corpse

The children stand by your bed
like fingers: middle, index, ring, little.
Two of them hold hands because
I have brought them to hear the corpse speak.

I could explain it, the amalgam
that makes a person, but the corpse insists.
Lips, almost resting, glimpse of teeth,
say *leave this with me.*

So I give them the catastrophe.
Doomed flesh. Death's porcelain
teaching movement by stillness.
They inhale it all. Sense

in an instant what is missing.
All that is good is gone, what is good is holy,
what is gone is the breath, so the breath is holy.
The breath,

which likes to travel
under an hereditary title,
is gone. The spirit scoffs
at sables and visitations.

This is what I lay at their door,
as a cat gives a dead mouse,
a source of joy. Sole source
for the six of us.

Half-life

'Two weeks,' and then a gesture, of hand and wrist,
like a duck diving,
like the opposite of exponential.
'In the end, the end,' we say, 'was fast like this.'

Serum on a raw shin,
juice on a cut peach,
drops from a broken washer:
the terms should bead like this.

Unsaid, the terms amass
as an obese person,
imprisoned in their own home, repeating,
'How did this happen?'

We broke the black bread,
would share one half
and save the rest.
Until we dealt in crumbs.

Cruelty has a half-life.
You were the half-life of his harshness.

Grandpa's itch for tears,
I never saw him fail
to hurt you.

Meals became small,
until they were no meals at all.
Until they were a new tradition,
sad as Christmas.

'Mother, mother,' we said,
to make you one.

A constellation unfigured,
parts but not their sum.

Two weeks ago you sat, sipping on the absolute
(bring out the best, though no one said it)
blue burned to brown – it was the cocktail hour.

Success too is a form of distance.
The lift chimed for the top floor,
doors dragged open on the marble foyer.

You led me, as if we were in the musée,
to see the strands of man untwisted,

to Grandpa in his desk chair.
He had laid out first a sheet of plastic.

My heirlooms: an oil painting and an ancient denunciation
carried like a mark on silver.

Each word whetted or withheld – coins tossed my way –
I kept them.

I'll build the archetype
with belly wax.
The work is sweet and makes me sleepy.
Each prismatic cell with a mother in it.
Women buried in honey.

I lay beside you on your Egyptian bed,
snug as a foetus, bound by your breath.

And the moon that white donkey waited.

The Last Sense

What is winter uncoupled from spring?
Pleasures shrivel where they hang.
Except speech, a clutch of words each day.

Then this – my cheek
on your chest.
Touch is the last sense.

Frozen leeks and chicken bones,
rows of unopened yoghurt,
and your scent about the place

like a last guest.
Linger – a directive –
don't let me.

Young Women in the Garden, Bonnard (1921–23/1945–46)

In this picture Renée is still
the age she was
that summer.

The summer it no longer mattered
how many
summers we have

She is still the age she was
when he loved her
when he left her
when her parents buried her.

Young Women in the Garden II/The Colour of Escape

Today he is reworking the image,
he is adding gold
to a painting of two women in a garden.

Today he is reworking the image
because some images are not easy
to leave, to finish,

could lead a man even to
smuggle a brush
into a gallery.

Is this how lovers retouch?
A dot of ochre,
a stroke of yellow.

Today he is reworking the image.
He is adding gold to this picture
which remains in his studio

as he, of the three,
remains in the world.
He is adding a golden headdress

or maybe a halo
to the younger woman,
something to protect her.

But halos
always come too late.
He is adding gold, I have said,

but you might call it a dirty yellow.
Yellow, colour of escape.
For whom, I do not know.

Aphrodite Genetyllis
Protectress of births

Paper Lantern

for my children

I kept my head
in a Chinese paper lantern,

lined my hollow
with the bones

of small pets
and other enthusiasms

and I have lived
invertedly

heart over brain.
Forgive me.

But I can carry,
perhaps was born to it.

My heart is an ass
and it has four hooves

clip clop, it goes
clip clop, clip clop.

Skoliosi

for Eliza

The Yasawans make
segmented fish from wood,
each piece, sliced to perfection,
so it moves
like the real thing,
          swerving off in a flicked slew

Hatchling,   forgive
these inch-long screws.

Undo

First, your pain, *like being on meat hooks.*
Next, each false assurance:
normal, normal, normal, normal.

Put the outsize screen to sleep – white snake –
let us unsee it.

Dismantle the table where they stretched you,
attach the springs they used onto our sneakers.

Back to the peculiar studio, this time I tell him,
'No.' I hand you back your clothes.

Sequences like funnels, doors like valves,
you hand me trust, I hand you up.

Unawake and unasleep, unspeaking courses
down your cheeks.

Undo Aaron's miracle –
unbend
and staff us comfort still.

Child Receding

to my son William

Out of the pond and up the hill you go,
pocket Olympian.
Leave me as a lizard tail

lying on the wintergreen.
Above us poplars gossip in the breeze.
Spend their silver dollars freely on the wind again.

The afternoon heat wanes.
The sun is teasing, cloud-coy.
I wait, supplicant

for one more
moment of warmth, that I may
leave in blaze.

Welcome to the Future of Custom Lightsabers

Every three days they offer me sabers
because you are eleven and you are my baby.
Single Blade, Deal of the Day, Free Grab Bag, Free T-shirt.

Every three days they offer me sabers
because we have one tilt
and this is where I am in it.

Ob.

An apostrophe on blotted sheets,
I wake, stainless.
Milk of amnesia is drained.
Weeds of longing for my deliverer
grow in its place.
'There will be nights,' he said,
leaning back in his chair.
But it's by day I see
the slender hawthorn tree.
Its bonny bloom, its crimson haw
and all year its blackish thorn.
In its branches a mynah sits.
It sports my beak, my perfect claws.

A Narrow Field

Open, the coffin shocked me.
I had thought that we were more disposed
to keep things hidden.
Thought – *I did not tick this box?*
In any case, you looked well

wearing the clothes I'd chosen –
light, comfortable linen, a touch of colour.
As per the regulations
there was no one there.
Still, the choice had vexed me.

You wore your hair as a small cloud
with the promise of showers
and I patted it as a child might
size up a stick of floss.
I saw you as a great painting

recovered from a cave or cellar
with me the expert
able to recognise the original.
Bohr said that an expert
is a man who has made

all the mistakes
in a narrow field.
And probably I have made

mistakes on you.
Inside the coffin, a sable curtain

and two pink buds,
my infant fists,
tangled inside it. Tangled
in that way babies have
of grabbing, and I mean really

yanking, their mother's hair.
The trick being
to stay calm,
even as a tear pricks.
So the baby knows it is not a game

which would only lead to more yanking.
The trick being to stay calm
as you unsnarl yourself
hair by hair
from their grasp.

Acknowledgements

I would like to thank the editors of the magazines, newspapers and anthologies in which some of these poems first appeared, sometimes in slightly different versions.

The Age: 'Ob.'; *Australian Poetry Journal*: 'MH17' and 'Nothing is Past'; *Australian Poetry Anthology*: 'A Clean House' and 'Egg'; *Canberra Times*: 'Skoliosi'; *foam:e*: 'A Party on the Coast'; *Island*: 'The Memory of Water'; *The Moth*: 'A Narrow Field'; *PN Review*: 'He Rises', 'Pothos II', 'Pothos III', and 'Yew'; *The Poetry Review*: 'A Clean House', 'True in the Senses' and 'Helens of Troy'; *Poetry d'Amour Anthology*: 'Camera Obscura'; *Shearsman*: '*Dora and the Minotaur* (1936) ink, pencil and scratching on paper'; *Stilts*: 'Undo'; *Westerly*: 'Market Day'.

'Egg' won the Ros Spencer Poetry Prize, 'Child Receding' won the Peter Cowan Writers' Centre Patrons' Prize for Poetry and 'The Memory of Water' was awarded the Gwen Harwood Poetry Prize.

Many thanks to Lisa Gorton for her encouragement and her editing, to Aleesha Paz, Ivor Indyk and all at Giramondo for their support, to Brook Emery for his guidance and to my family.

About the author

Amy Crutchfield studied Classics and Law at the University of Melbourne. Her poetry has been published in Australia, the UK and Ireland. She has worked as a teacher and a lawyer. *The Cyprian* is her first book.